Rhythms of My Heart

Rhythms of My Heart

Celebrating Fifty with Poetry

Volume 1

Cynthia Grenyion

CONCLUSIO
HOUSE PUBLISHING

Copyright © 2016 by Cynthia Grenyion

All rights reserved. This book or any portion thereof may not be reproduced or used in any manner whatsoever without the express written permission of the publisher except for the use of brief quotations in a book review.

Printed in Canada
First Printing, 2016

ISBN 9780994920430

Published by:
Conclusio House Publishing
503-7700 Hurontario Street
Suite 209
Brampton, ON
L6Y 4M3

www.conclusiohouse.com

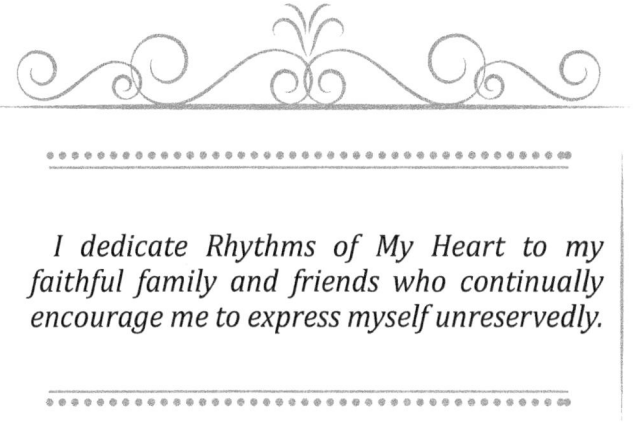

I dedicate Rhythms of My Heart to my faithful family and friends who continually encourage me to express myself unreservedly.

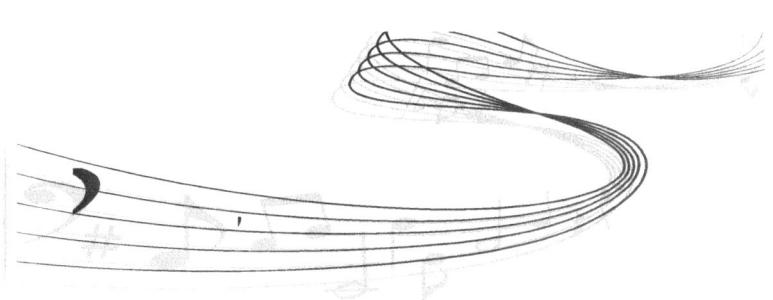

Introduction

Rhythms of My Heart reveals the deep emotions of a Christian woman who wears the hat of a pastor's wife, a motivational speaker, an educator, child evangelist, and children's writer. She experienced mental, emotional, and social struggles in her youth, but believed in the supernatural power of God and the frankness of her admittances to overcome the realities of her situation.

She elevates poetry and prose to a new dimension where she opens her heart to spill her guts to her God about certain issues in order to cultivate a positive attitude and to unleash her undeniable prowess in creativity. In her fascination with love, friendship, life, nature, and culture, she unlocks her heart to express gratitude and reveal the nuances and disturbances that life gives through her voice of poetry, in celebration of her *fiftieth birthday.*

It was the author's plan to compile fifty poems in recognition of the years of her age, but through divine inspiration she realized that her collection of poetry has sixty-six poems as the Bible of her faith has sixty-six books. In her collection, there is raw truth and revelation that solicit change for our souls.

Her utterances were inspired by real experiences, triggered by real emotions, and stirred by real desires. These poems were released to motivate, educate, and empower others who struggle but have a mind to excel against the odds.

Table of Contents

I Celebrate God 1
There is No Reason 3
Rosebuds and Sweetness 4
Thank Him 5
What if 6
He Knows, Just Call on His Name 7
His Voice 9
God, You are Always There 10
Shake Off 11
God Gives Life 12
I Know He Loves Me 13
A Love Tested, A Love You Can Trust 15
Rhythms of Love: Love is…Love Causes 18
Love that Speaks 20
Love in Reverse 22
Love is Something If … 24
Wife to husband: Writing to the One I Love 26
Husband to Wife: Replying to the one I love 27
Loving you 28
The Morning Kiss 29
Love 30
The Golden Touch of Love 32
I Think of You 34

I Am in Love with Love: Watching lovers 35
Fallen in Love 36
Love on Valentine's Day 38
Valentine's Surprise 39
Rhythms of Nature 42
The View Through My Window 45
Oh Butterfly, Oh Butterfly 47
Nature Speaks 49
A Mother's Heart 50
A Mother's Reflection 52
Mediocrity 54
I Belong to the Kingdom 56
Trapped 58
I Am Not Trapped 59
The Rainbow's Promise 61
Faithful Friend 62
God's Eyes 63
The Gift of Love 65
Love Doesn't Leave You 67
I Pause to Say 68
His Clear Voice 69
I Will See You Later 70
When I See Him Again: A Young Love's Story 71
Be Aware 73
If You Are in Love 75
Rhythms of Culture 77
Church People Have Different Faces 78

Behold, Your Sins Shall Find You Out	80
Oh God, We Are Guilty	82
The Girl, Diamond, Next Door	84
Shifted Rear	87
Cockroach Nuh Business in a Fowl Fight	90
Gossip	92
Rhythms of the Park	94
Gullies Cry	96
Nothing You Say or Do	99
I Want To	100
Break the Silence (In Memory of a Student)	102
Tribute to My Mentor, My Queen, Dr Smikle	105
Tribute to Myles Munroe	107
A Look at Death	108
The Power of Death	109
Dying	110
My Prayer	111

I Celebrate God!

I celebrate God for the moments that I experience on Earth.
I celebrate time that extends to
fifty seconds,
fifty minutes,
fifty hours,
fifty days,
fifty weeks,
fifty months,
fifty years!
I celebrate the joys, the tears.
I celebrate God for planning my life,
I celebrate my family and my friends,
I celebrate my achievements.
I celebrate the time I spend on Earth,
The seconds,
the minutes,
the hours,
the days,
the months,
fifty years
that I share,
right here on planet Earth,
I celebrate God for my physical birth,
I celebrate God for my spiritual birth.
I celebrate God for all my friends,
 I celebrate God without limits.
My celebration extends to
seconds,

minutes,
hours,
days,
weeks,
months,
years.
Friends, create a balance and celebrate God for the joys and the tears today.

There Is No Reason

Hi out there!
I am a Black, Christian, Caribbean woman, who is proud to be one.
One of my heroes is Maya Angelou,
She uses words to inspire, educate, and silence her foes.
There is no reason you should walk with your eyes on your toes,
There is no reason you should think that your destiny will be woes,
There is no reason to be sour with life,
There is no reason to fuss for not being a wife.
There is no reason you should not love your children and teach them good morals diligently,
There is no reason you should try to stop me from being me,
There is no reason you should stop praying from your knee,
You see, we women are familiar with pain and hurt of some sorts,
We know what it is to be alone and cry tears and have worried thoughts,
We have hopes, we have dreams, and we have dignity and certainly integrity,
We know how to work, fight, create, and "tun wi han fi mek fashion" for productivity.
There is no reason to doubt; be confident and speak out.
There is reason for me to shout,
I am a free Black, Christian, Caribbean woman!

Rosebuds and Sweetness

When you think of roses, what comes to your mind?
When you think of sweetness, what do you think of?
Well, I have had a beautiful encounter, one to remember,
A special day when I celebrated my birthday,
My friends came, all so happy and cheery,
Soon they were gone, and I gazed at the remaining beauty before me.

Rosebuds and sweetness were erected in the middle of my hall,
Ready to be consumed by my family, all ready for a ball,
There was the reminder of my youth, fifty.
"I am not a pup," I thought, "I am half a century."
Three layers of cake were decorated with sunshine yellow, cream, and deep red roses,
I tasted it, and it melted in my mouth in deep caresses,
I smiled and took a bite of the roses,
It sank deep in the sweetness, and it melted away.
Again and again, I was indulging for a moment—
White icing sweet, carrot cake so sweet, red roses so rare
To put on a few pounds I did not fear.
I made up my mind to enjoy my day to the max,
"I do not have a care in the world. I have to pay no tax.
More sweetness, more roses to devour this very hour,
This is my day. I will have to do less next year."
I consumed the sweetness, and now I can only reminisce on the beauty
I saw and ate.
Sweetness with rosebuds,
Rosebud sweetness!

Thank Him

There are many ungrateful people around,
Who walk around town with a frown.
They receive things from God and others,
And act as if they produce them with their own powers.
They seem to have a load on their backs,
They are ready to give you an attack.
They complain, ridicule, and are naturally vexed,
I denounce their sour spirit of ungratefulness.

God expects us to show thankfulness
For all the things we possess.
We should have a positive attitude to thank God for the air we breathe,
To thank him for the sunshine and the rain,
To thank him for the sorrow and the pain,
To thank him for his faithfulness,
To thank Him for taking us from our mess,
To thank Him for the food He provides,
To thank him for the clothes we wear,
To thank him for good health and peace,
To thank him for the shelter and ease.

Thank him for the people in our lives,
Thank him for the husbands and the wives,
Thank Him for the friends and the foes,
Thank him if you are rich or poor.
When we are thankful we please God more,
He builds our character for us to cope.
Be thankful, smile and do not mope,
You can have a grateful heart.
The right thing to do now is to start.

What If...

What if I was from a different race?
What if I had life easy?
What if I did not have to work?
What if I was born of different parents?
What if I was rich?
What if I was living in a different place?
What if I was a male and not a female?
What if I was not married?
What if I was not a Christian?
What if...?

What if I could tell you all I know about you?
What if I could be there with you?
What if you were dead?
What?
What!
It will always be what ifs.

I am happy to be born of my parents.
I am comfortable though I am poor.
I am pleased that I am here.
I am grateful that I am Black.
I am satisfied that life is difficult.
I am content that I am married.
I am elated that I am a Christian
I accept that I cannot be there with you.
I am thankful to be alive.
I am happy to be me.

What if you were not you?
What would you be?
What if...?

He Knows:
Just Call on His Name

I know you are hurting and you want to leave where you are,
I know you are blurting and asking why God chose this thing to happen to you,
I know you feel confused and broken inside,
I know you are troubled because you really don't know what to do,
Just call on His name, "Jesus."
Call on His name,
He brings you peace,
Joy and satisfaction,
Call on His name to relieve you from shame.

He knows the pain you feel,
He knows the sorrow of your heart,
He knows how you wish you could disappear,
He knows that you are scared,
He knows that you feel unprepared,
He knows that you feel like a fish out of water,
He knows that you are pondering all matters for better,
He knows.
Just call His name, "Jesus," and trust Him with all of your heart.

Trust Him to take all the broken pieces apart,
Then put all the broken pieces together,
Whatever He does is not for the better but for the best.

Rest assured that He will help you win the test,
Call on the name, "Jesus."
He will cushion you from headaches and heartaches.
He knows that you want to be out,
He knows that people are telling your story about,
He knows that you are poised for a breakthrough,
He knows that you need not convince the crowd, but the few,
He knows that you are His miracle,
He knows you are not concerned with the spectacular,
He knows ...
Just call on his name.

His Voice

His voice makes a difference,
When He speaks He relieves my troubled mind.
His voice makes a difference,
When He speaks He encourages my heart.
His voice lifts my spirit to praise Him,
His voice establishes me to stand in Him.
He said He will never leave nor forsake me,
He said He will be a hiding place and a present help,
He said, "I will be your peace
And your comforter."
He said He will be a strong tower,
He said, "I am the great I Am,
I will be what you want Me to be."
He said, "You have the ability to conquer."
He said He will take me on His shoulder.
He said, "Listen to My voice in the war,
Listen to my voice in the wind,
Listen to my voice in the waves,
Listen to my voice in the water,
Listen to my voice in the flower,
Listen to my voice in the creature,
I control all, I am Creator."
His voice makes a difference,
He brings a settled peace to my soul.

God, You Are Always There

God, you are always there,
You are always within my fears.
God, you are always amidst my tears.
You are always there when I feel alone,
You are always there when I cannot speak,
You are always there when I feel so weak,
You are always there to give my heart good cheer,
You are always there when I make a mistake,
You are there to let me know I do not need to fake,
You are always there through my heartaches and pain,
You are always there to help me know my health I can regain,
You are always there when I have uncertainties,
You are always there when I have my calamities,
You are always there to lift my hands up high,
You are always there when I have to say to my friends, "Goodbye."
You are always there when I struggle to keep from sin,
You are always there encouraging me to help me win,
You are always there to dispel all my doubts,
You are always there, despite the fact that I am always about,
You are always there.
You are always there, my Love.
You are always there, my God.
You are always there, Omnipresent One.
You are always there when I feel numb,
Disappointed,
Sad,
You are always there, so I can trust You.
You are forever faithful!

Shake Off

Shake off the disappointments,
Shake off the ashes,
Shake off the condemnation,
Shake off the disillusionment,
Shake off the torment,
Shake off the illness,
Shake off the possessiveness,
Shake off the mess,
Shake off the stress,
Shake off the addiction,
Shake off the disturbances,
Shake off the negativities,
Shake off the pessimism,
Shake off the criticism,
Shake off the crowded thoughts,
Shake off the poverty,
Shake off the distresses,
Shake off the hypocrisy,
Shake off the false expectations,
Shake off your limitations,
Shake off the worries.
Shake off and put on life,
Life abundantly,
Successful life,
God's life in you!

God Gives Life

God gives life to the ones who are discouraged.
God gives life to poor and sad hearts.
God gives life to the sick and hopeless.
God gives life to the addicted soul.
God gives life to the weak and fragile child.
God gives life to the lonely mom and the confused dad.
God gives life to the single parent.
God gives life to the man in chains.
God gives life to the imprisoned mind.
God gives life to the insane.
God gives life to the dead situation.
God gives life to the hungry man in the home.
God gives life to the old woman who doesn't know her own.
God gives life to the offended.
God gives life to the suffering patient.
God gives life to the special indigent.
God gives life to you.
God gives life to me!

I Know He Loves Me

It is good to feel loved, wanted, and appreciated.
I really do not know anyone who doesn't love to feel loved, wanted, and appreciated.
Feelings fail us at times, they move passionately from uncertain, like, dislike, love, hate,
And sometimes to frustration and disappointment,
But to know you are loved is great.
You don't have to guess, you don't have to wonder,
You don't have to doubt, you don't have to worry,
You don't have to pretend to love Him when you don't,
He is all-knowing.
He knows the measure of your love,
He wants your love unreservedly.
I know He loves me,
He loves me regardless of my situation,
My limitations,
My location,
My colour,
My ideas,
My preferences,
He loves you and me.
I am not saying I feel,
I am saying I know He loves me.
He loves me beyond what I am able to express,
He gave up all, sacrificially, so that I can be loved,
Wanted,
Appreciated.

My soul is valuable, and I am so special to die for.
He died for me to have peace and satisfaction.
I know He loves me.
Who among us would die for someone?
Who among us would love someone with their sins and not destroy them instantly?
Who would ever love us when we are so wicked and spiteful?
Who among us loves without expecting anything in return?
Which one of us would love Him sacrificially?
Who among us would love without complaining?
Who among us would love beyond boundaries and borders?
Who would love as the God-book teaches—"let us love one another, forgiving one another"?
Who among us would say, "I am tired of being loved, wanted, and appreciated"?
I really do not care if anyone bothers.
Are we our brother's keeper?
I am loved, wanted, and appreciated.
I know He loves me.

A Love Tested, A Love You Can Trust

Sacrificial, selfless love,
A love you can trust,
A love tested on the altar and on a cross—
A symbol of love for all human beings.
Abraham was willing to sacrifice his son,
He felt the pain of parting with his only one,
He wondered why he would have to give up his only son,
He looked for an opportunity to run.
Yet he made an altar and decided to sacrifice to experience God's approval.
He was willing to show his commitment and to show the glory of self-denial.
He said to Abraham, "Now I know you love Me, your action is counted as righteousness."
A love tested, selfless love,
Unconditional love.
God was willing to sacrifice His only Son,
He saw the people's need for salvation.
He looked at the cross, He looked at the nation,
He said, "Let this cup pass from me."
He felt the loss of friends in the garden,
He knew he would be denied and betrayed.
Yet He said, "Nevertheless, not as I will but as you will, oh God."
The proclamation came to show victory in His resurrection,
And upon our trust in Him we will experience inspiration.

It is because of the love He had,
Selfless, sacrificial love, tested.
It is like Abraham's love on the altar,
It is like Jesus dying on the cross,
A love tested on the altar and on a cross—
A symbol of love for all human beings,
Sacrificial, selfless love,
A love you can trust.
What will you give up for Him?

Rhythms of Love

Love is... Love causes

Love is the strongest feeling anyone on earth can experience.
It looks beyond the straight nose, nice fragrance, big house, lovely clothes,
Beautiful speeches, bright brains, it goes beyond our wildest imagination.
There are different rhythms of love
Love is the strongest connection between friends, couples,
children and their pets,
mommy and daddy,
and family.
There are different rhythms of love
Love causes you to move away from the stereotypes of expression to being quiet,
And allows the heart to speak, the eyes to say it, the soul to know it, and the lips to feel it.
Love is the finest thread that wraps the gift of human beings.
It is covered with sweet kisses, hugs, merry hearts, and hopeful anticipations.
Love causes people to fight through their hurts together, to claim each other to be forever.
Love ignites the relationship, regardless of the years in between, and makes you try at all times not to be mean.
It motivates you to show your emotion each time something reminds you of someone you love,
It brings a smile that releases the pain and stirs your

devotion.
There are different rhythms of love
When you love you might try to hide it, but love that is true always seeps through the eyes of the soul.

The unspoken words of the heart, the union of the body, the unwrapping of gifts, the heartfelt throb of hopes, and illusive pleasures of your dreams.

Love is great, and sometimes people might think it is fate.

Loves causes you to know that love is destiny and will last for all eternity.

Love that Speaks

I often think that every word speaks to our soul, whether we are young or old.
When I think of the words we use, I realize that each triggers some kind of emotion,
Triggers some need for reflection, some kind of memory, some kind of person, some type of idea, some kind of experience.
Whatever LOVE speaks,
Love speaks to my heart lovingly,
Love speaks to my heart deeply,
Love speaks to me in a whisper,
Love speaks in a flicker,
Loves speaks unconsciously,
It speaks to me loudly.
As I see images, reflections on the faces of lovers,
As I see people worship in God's presence,
As I see our children play with their favourite toys,
As I see families making sacrifices for each one to reach their goals,
As I see sports athletes wave their country flags,
As I see the wide smiles of successful graduates,
As I see the proud parents screaming their children's names,
LOVE speaks.
Love speaks to my heart as I feel the heartbeat of my friend,
Love speaks to me deeply as I feel my heart tug at my soul,
Love speaks to me in a whisper as the tear wells in my eyes,

Love speaks in a flicker when the tear falls on my cheeks,
Love speaks to me unconsciously when a smile tugs at my lips,
Love speaks to me when I turn and his name is the first on my mind,
Love speaks to me loudly as I make a satisfied sigh.
LOVE speaks.

Love in Reverse

I reflect on the song that I sing with my children at church,
It is love that makes the world go round,
You make the world go round,
I make the world go round,
It is love that makes the world go round, so let us pass it on to everyone.
It is love that makes the world go round.
Love without weight is what we call hate.
We often pass on hate.
Hate kills love,
Hate suffocates the potential of love,
Hate diminishes the value of love,
Hate crushes the pure passion to love,
And hate cracks the vessel of love and leaks the sinews of substance from the intentions of the mind and soul.
Hate eats the soul slowly like termite in a wood,
And acts like the explosive of a weapon,
And presses flat the pulp of hope,
And squeezes the flesh to deep pain,
And wrings tightly the chords of love to brokenness.
Hate hits with great vigour and toughens the heart to callousness and bitterness.
Hate destroys the fragrance and becomes like repellent to kill the parasites,
Hate covers and distorts the plan of God for your life and will cause you to detest your wife.
Hate pushes you to the peak of no return and leads you to stupor and to use a knife.
Hate creeps in your soul like a heated iron over a

long time and makes you its victim,
And you become like a big monster, a giant like Goliath.
But love in reverse will destroy hate, bring life to the potential of love.
Love increases the value of love,
Love raises the passion to love,
Love seals the wounds and collects the sinews of life,
Love nourishes your soul like nutrients to your body,
It acts like a repellant to destroy the parasites that hate causes—
Envy, jealousy, malice, and pride.
Love nurtures hope and massages the mind to think positively.
Love touches lightly and softens your heart to forgiveness and restoration,
Love covers a multitude of sins and activates the plan of God in our lives,
And allows us to love everyone and not find a weapon.
Love pushes you to think before you return with an angry word or tool,
And leads to the pasture of righteousness because you know the golden rule and you are no fool.
It is love that makes the world go round.
It's you and it's me that make the world go round.
Love without weight is what we call hate.
We often pass on hate.
It's not too late to have love in reverse.

Love Is Something If...

If you give it away it comes right back to you,
Love is like a magical penny,
If you spend it or give it away it comes right back to you.
Share a smile and it's contagious,
Wear a new fashion and you get attention,
Put on a delicate, musky perfume and your fragrance fills the room,
Laugh raucously or deeply, an amusing chuckle,
Fight to get to the front of a crowd to get assistance,
Call out loudly that you are selling only one broom,
Love a child and make a funny face,
There will be different responses
To the smile,
To the fashion,
To the fragrance,
To the laughter,
To the fight,
To the call,
And to love.
Some will frown at you and wonder what there is to smile about,
Some might think that you are weird and old for such a fashion,
Some might sneeze at your expensive aroma,
Some might have no sense of humour and ridicule you for being real,
Some might think you are undisciplined to go in front to be served,
Some in hearing your call to sell a broom might look at you and think that the broom you are selling is used,

Some might think your love is not genuine and want to investigate why you love,
And for the child, he or she might even cry.
Regardless of the response,
We should love everyone sincerely,
Despite how they look,
What they wear,
How they smell,
Where they are,
What they do,
What they say,
What they think.
When we love, it will come right back to us.
It might not come back from the person you love,
But if you love everyone every day, it will come right back to you in a different way.
Love is like a magical penny,
If we give it away, it will come right back to you and me.

Wife to Her Husband: Writing to the One I Love

I love you, but you are far, far, far away.
I love you, and I want to see you again, I pray.
I look at the sea, and as vast as it is, so is my love for you,
As deep as the ocean, so is my love for you.
As wide as the sea, so my hands are ready to give you an embrace,
As far as my eyes could see across the horizon, so my love has no boundaries.
I love you so much,
I speak to my heart and body to make a hush,
I go back to places we usually go and rekindle the memories,
 Come to me now, I want to renew our sacred vow.
My heart aches within me,
You are too far away.
I love you, and I want to see you again, I pray.
I take your things and smell them to keep your scent,
I read and re-read all the messages you've sent to me,
I repeat the words you've said, over and over again,
But it is not the same.
There is a steady rising pain,
My eyes are misty, my body fails,
And my heart cries out to you,
When will I see you again?

Husband to Wife:
Replying to the One I love

My love, I know that you miss me.
I know you want me by your side.
I know you wish to change our circumstances,
But we know that God will hasten the time for us to meet.
I think about our sweet reunion and your smile and the sweet bed union.
I cry to be where I should be,
I am tempted many times to quit so I can be with you,
But I know being here is the best for us,
So let our love grow and ensure that we please God at all times.
Remember, my love, you will soon be here for me to massage your feet.
Honey, my sweet one, one day we will surely meet.
Put your mind on the work you do,
Find a child to help along the way,
Go to the women's meeting and be occupied,
Read God's Word and get intimate with Him.
I love you, my loving wife,
My kisses are here for you,
I keep my lips moist for you to touch,
My body is secured only for you to explore.
I pray that one day soon I will see you at my front door.

Loving You

Loving you brings me freedom,
Loving you brings me peace,
Loving you brings me comfort,
Loving you brings me satisfaction.
When I love you I smile freely,
When I love you my fear diminishes,
When I love you I touch me unashamed,
When I love you I sense the meaning of deep devotion.
Loving you makes me understand unconditional love.
You told me that it is not what I have that causes you to love me, you said it is who I am.
I really have to love you because you never cared about my possessions.
It is easy for me to love you because you always listen to my foolish dreams and encourage me beyond my fantasies.
Loving you helps me see my limitations and realize it is best to love the one who loves me most and will give me no reason to fear being exposed.
Loving you teaches me to forgive others as you forgive me and my fantasies,
And leads me to see myself as I reflect on God's Word.
Loving you gives me a sense of belonging, a spirit of comfort, and a settled peace within,
Loving you keeps me free from sin.

The Morning Kiss

I stretched my hands towards him, he refused,
I stretched my legs, he did the same,
I stretched my lips towards him, he moved closer,
and he looked deeply in my eyes and gave me a morning kiss that
revived me,
pushed me,
sobered me,
raised me,
loved me.
I held his face with my nervous hands and kissed him back, fervently, caressingly, greatly, and lovingly,
I stretched my hands towards him, and he hugged me, tightly.
I stretched my legs, and he received them gladly.
His eyes smiled at me, and I felt l his lips release in a smile from the morning kiss.

Love

L-ively heart
O-pen spirit
V-ibrant encounter
E-nthralling experience,
The heart skips a beat and throbs at the rhythm of one's soul.
The heart becomes lively as they draw close, close, closer.
Both hearts now do a call and response beat.
It is sweet, it gives a repeat, their eyes dance and sparkle, and their smiles communicate what they want to say.
Their hearts are lively as they beat the rhythm of their souls.
Their spirits embrace each other.
They chuckle nervously and speak foolish nothings as they draw close, **close**, **closer.**
Their spirits rise to look at each other in a fun-like manner, and they share feather kisses to the eyelashes, the nose tips, the cheeks, the chins, to the lips, and their spirits fly openly together to explore the contours of their faces.
Their hearts and spirits combine to give them a vibrant encounter. Their hands move around and their legs anchor as they get close, close, **closer.**
His hands grip her back and her hands explore the taut muscles of his shoulders.
Their lips are sealed as expressed messages flash in

their minds.

Their minds are seared with deep emotions that push them to deep reverence, ready for deep devotion.

Their hearts, spirits, minds, and souls emerge with the urge to reach the highest summit.

Their souls hold each other with passion beyond what they can control.

Their hearts beat lively, their spirits beg openly, their souls pivot vibrantly, and their bodies ignite devotedly to an enthralling experience as they become close, **close**, **closer.**

The Golden Touch of Love

Dedicated to children with cancer

In the hospital room, the nurse looked at her young patient and prayed silently in her heart for the sick girl's recovery. She combed her hair, which was falling out, fed her with spoonful after spoonful of cereal, and nodded approvingly as the child made efforts to chew and swallow.

She whispered her name and the fragile hands touched the nurse, and a small, quivering smile stayed on her lips as she said, "Thank you," and moved her little hands in small circles at the top of the nurse's hands. The nurse stopped and put away the cereal and covered her hands with her hand, then they both looked down at their hands and fittingly clasped them together.

It was a golden touch, the love they both felt for each other changed the atmosphere.

The little girl sat upright and said loud and clear. "I love you, Jesus, and think your touch is a touch of love."

Then the nurse spoke with tears rolling down her eyes. "I touched you because I love you. I touched you because I have no little girl to touch. My little girl died of leukemia many years ago. I touched you as Jesus would have touched you. I prayed that my hands would be like Jesus so you will be totally healed."

The little girl answered, "Nurse, when I was holding your hand, I was holding the hands of Jesus. He said 'I love you,' and He showed me His hands with the

two nail scars to prove His love for me."
The nurse replied, "What you are saying?"
"I saw Jesus in my sleep. I think it was a sleep. He put food in my mouth, touched me, raised me up, and said, just like he told Jairus's daughter, 'Rise and be healed.' When I opened my eyes, I saw you, nurse. You are Jesus. I am healed, nurse!"
The nurse looked at the other nurses and sick children who heard the weak voice that was now loud and clear. "Surely, you are healed, my little one. Your faith has made you whole. You have gotten a golden touch of love, a touch from Jesus."
"Nurse, my hair may go, but Jesus loves me. Everyone can see my face clearly. I do not have to bother about hair combing, hair styles, and hair accessories. Jesus gave me a golden touch. I am healed from the inside, so I will wear a smile all the time.

I Think of You

I think of you and wonder if you think about me,
I think of you working,
And I wonder if you are idling,
I think of you sleeping,
And I wonder if you were dreaming,
I think of you believing,
And I wonder if you are understanding,
I think of you reading,
And I wonder if you are writing,
I think of you singing,
And I wonder if you are thinking,
I think of you speaking,
And I wonder if you are rehearsing,
I think of you.
I wonder if you are happy.
I miss you!

I Am In Love With Love: Watching Lovers

I am in love with love.
I watch lovers exchange smiles unashamed,
Even if they have only gums or a few teeth.
I watch lovers hold hands and whisper each other's names.
I watch lovers look into each other's eyes,
Not looking for matter, some scar.
I watch lovers walk down the aisles.
I watch lovers walking together as stars.
I watch lovers speak their hearts' vows,
Meaning every word they say.
I watch lovers pose to take pictures.
I watch lovers kneeling in prayer.
I watch lovers forget the trivial things to gaze at each other.
I watch lovers be all they can be for each other.
I watch lovers touch each other and hug tightly.
I watch lovers take a small gift like a petal of a flower.
I watch lovers wait on each other, despite the long hours.
I watch lovers act like they have not a care in the world.
I watch lovers walking in the park,
Gazing at lights and scenes in the dark.
I am in love with love.
Love is as strong as death.
Love takes away my breath.

Fallen in Love

I smile and see your smile in reply,
And my heart melts away like the snow.
I look at you and my heart skips and frolics in my stomach.
I touch your hands and the feeling vibrates through my veins,
Through my fingers,
Through me.
I look and touch
And feel so much in love… in love with you,
I've fallen in love.
Will you help me up?
I have fallen.
I smile,
I look,
I feel,
I am in love with you!

I smile again, and you smile away the pain,
And my heart simmers in silence remembering your name.
I gaze at your lips,
And I long for you to reply with a kiss.
I touch your face, and you look at me deeply
And sigh and hug me very tightly.
No word, no explanation, only emotion,
You have fallen too.
I see it in your smiles,
Your touch,

Your eyes,
We have fallen in love.
If being up will cause it to go, then I will remain fallen.
I am in love, so much in love with you.
I smile,
I look,
I feel,
I've fallen in love,
So much in love with you.

Love on Valentine's Day

Love is the most beautiful thing on the earth,
On Valentine's Day we think of love and not hurt.
I send my love to my family and friends.
My love is flavoured sweetly without pretense.
We might be far away but you are still near,
We might not talk often but I still care.
I love you, and today I need an ocean of paper to express how much.
I love you today on Valentine's Day,
And when the day has passed, I will love you even more.
I am glad love can be expressed by the be rich and the poor.
I pray constantly that God will bring you peace and success,
I crave to be close by you in order to let you know.
I guess I will be better able to express my emotion as I grow.
I wish you showers of love on Valentine's Day.
I wish you love beyond a day.
I love you for each tomorrow when you are sick or in sorrow.
My love is not limited to a day,
I promise to love you forever.
The most powerful and excellent way is love.
The most wonderful and excellent way is love.
Love is amazing.

Valentine's Surprise

A surprise, at times, comes from a rare place
I went to a funeral reflecting sadly
I needed a phone so badly
My laptop was damaged and I had difficulty
Communicating effectively
I prayed for an updated phone
Prayed and left it there
I sought out to get one too
Then a stranger spoke with me for a brief moment
At the funeral get-together
A Few hours later she knocked on my door
And gave me a surprise—a new BLU phone
This is so rare, I felt very queer
I hugged her and said, "Thanks"
I laughed out loud and blew Jesus a kiss
This time He showed me that He doesn't miss
He knew my struggle to connect with others
And my desire to have 'WhatsApp' and other updated features
I must say that my God is a provider!
Though trivial you might think this is, the Lord knew my heart and gave me a BLU phone from the hand of a kind stranger
I am now learning about the apps and reading my Bible
Connecting with family and friends and other people
I knew it was God who whispered to this person
Who thought it fit to give me a miracle
On a special day where love flows freely

"Give my daughter a surprise," He told the stranger.
Today I am catching on, even though I believe I have very large fingers
The many errors I've made to friends in typing give me the jitters
Anyway, they, too, laughed and encouraged me
To enjoy the luxury of using BLU
Thank you, my friend, you are no longer a stranger
I appreciate you very much for
Blessing me with a Valentine's surprise.

Rhythms of Nature

Rhythms of Nature

On Nevis Mountain one early morn,
My friend, Dasent, gave me a call,
We travelled, talked on, joked on our way,
And met other friends to climb the trail,
We climbed, rested, enjoyed our way,
"We can conquer anything," we said that day.

On Nevis Mountain I experienced the rhythms of nature.
I actually climbed on ropes to see six amazing waterfalls. The falls are different,
Each has a different gush, colour, and depth of water, cascading from its heights.
I saw and felt more than I expected.
There was the wind whistling in the trees,
The awesome designs of flora blooming scented the air with aroma that keeps the atmosphere alive,
The fascinating existence of fauna—monkeys, rare birds, and insects took my breath away.
As we went further, higher on the winding tracks, and roped our way to the top,
There was a rush of excitement that elicited "oohs" and "aahs" from our lips,
These expressions were flowing like the falls from our hearts.
Songs and poetry flowed naturally as we enjoyed the shower on our skin and our faces,
We were wet and shivering to the cold rejuvenating freshness and we forgot all our distresses,

We chatted without inhibitions about the realities of life and the ecosystem's interdependence,
We took snapshots and explored, and treasured the memories of permanence.
I wish we could stay at the heights and relax in the beauty and tranquility,
I wish I could walk casually to capture the mountain falls and its unspoiled trickle.
The rocks looked like deep-red-stained mahogany with rugged designs curved by frequent baths.
The twisted thistles, massive trees trunks, and quaint patterned leaves created a canopy across the skies,
The sun peeped at us through the openings and massaged our faces and kissed our lips to say "Good morning."
We stopped several times and gazed in silent wonder at the greenery,
The sweet music from the birds punctuated the scenery,
We were awed by the natural wealth we beheld,
And my heart could not hold steady, my eyes became misty to behold the majestic creation.
The fellowship with new friends, nature lovers inspired and rejuvenated an inspiration for reflection.
As the guide from Adventure Tours spoke, I learned messages for success—
Keep focused,
Look up,
Look at the guide before you,
Put your weight on the rope,
Take little steps,
Look behind you
For the places to put your feet in,
Place your feet together,
Don't let go off the rope, even though it burns your hands,
You can do it.

After a difficulty or a victory, the tour guide clapped and praised us verbally.

I slipped a little at times, and he lifted me up again and encouraged me to push forward.

I know today you might be looking for a positive word to follow the trail in life.

Repeat the steps that the tour guide gave me as I climbed to reach the waterfalls.

Climb to success, you can do it.

Every time I open my doors I reflect on Adventure Tours on Nevis Mountain with the six fascinating falls.

The lesson learned is the journey to success.

The View from My Window
St Kitts-Nevis

Across the Caribbean Sea is the Queen of the Caribbean
In all its grandeur and pristine beauty.
There lies the spread blue splendour that ascends to the manicured hills,
There from my window is the creation of a breathtaking panoramic view.
The glistening waters of the sea
Look like sparkling crystals in all their glory,
Spectacular, clear, and majestic,
The hues of blue from aqua green, to navy blue, to light blue, and a mixture in between
Gives a variegated flash of sunlight against watery reflection.
I was mesmerized by God's design of perfection,
And the orange-yellow sunset glowed in the horizon,
The boats, both small and large, basking in the surroundings of ocean spray,
Each brings life far and near to the bay.
Through my window I see the lush green shrubs
And tall, elegant coconut trees swaying to the rhythms of the breeze,
The broad well-laden, fiery glory of the Poinciana transforms the atmosphere with its national beauty.
I watch the troupe of monkeys hopping happily in the tamarind trees, eating and chattering away, gleefully.
I see the brave birds chirping loudly, being disturbed by their hairy foes.

The postcard view is so perfect it dispels the darkness of the soul and relieves my daily woes.
I watch as the evening changes and the night comes revealing the sparkling lights of St Kitts,
The City of Gems.

Oh Butterfly, Oh Butterfly
Niagara Parks, Canada

Oh Butterfly, oh butterfly,
You are a beauty!
You did have a history,
Your first place was not pretty.
You've really forgotten your first state,
You looked so ugly,
But you stayed through the process until
Now you have colour,
You have wings.
You were a worm that could fly,
You knew your position was temporary crawling,
You knew that your appearance was temporary looking,
You knew that your movement was temporary slowing,
You knew that you had to go through a time of silence,
You knew you had to be covered with a new clothing,
You knew that when the time was right
You would have wings to fly,
You knew that you were the worm that had the potential to fly,
And you did!
You're a beauty, oh butterfly,
You move and rest lightly on the plants and drink from their nectar.
You are free to see, move, and be.
People are awed by you.
You look at the stages of the other caterpillars

And wait for them to go through the process of metamorphosis.
I watch as you alight on different surfaces,
Feeling sweet, knowing beauty and admiration from other creatures,
Beautiful patterns, majestic colours, oh so rare,
Oh, beautiful butterfly, don't mind me, I have to stare!

Nature Speaks

There are many contrasts in creation.
Silence,
Serenity,
Rush of life from creatures,
Soft chirping sounds in the distance,
Lullaby peace from the city,
Healing feeling from the calm sea in the evening,
Contrast of greens, burgundy red like sorrel and dusty grey
Shrubs decorated the paths,
Creating a scene
For reflection,
Recreation,
Romance.
There is a feeling of peace,
There is no need to be sad,
The darkness of my heart dispels,
The sun rises and cradles me with its rays.
Silence,
Serenity,
Tranquillity,
Rushes of life from creatures
In and out of trees,
There is a whisper in the breeze,
The coolness caresses my being,
Nature speaks to me.

A Mother's Heart

The baby cries to embrace the world,
Ready to know the happiness that life brings,
Listens to the birds chirping and to her mom who sings,
She is held by the strong arms of her dad,
And she thinks that there is nothing bad.
She coos, smiles,
Rolls over, poos,
She has nothing else to do,
She grows,
Creeps,
Stumbles many times,
Then she walks,
She imitates and talks,
And makes strong steps each day.
Then her world changes,
She hears the expletives,
She gets caught in mischief,
She feels the pain of the flame,
She touches and explores and knows rain,
She knows dirt,
She knows water,
She knows mud,
She knows crawling insects,
She plays and squeezes her toys,
She sees the similarities and the differences,
She eats and bites to get attention,
She knows how to choose what she likes and refuse

that which she doesn't.
No more a baby, a small infant ready for school,
Her world becomes larger,
With more people, enemies, and few friends,
She fights to survive,
She chooses what to be in her life,
She gets older,
Then soon the world changes again,
She realizes different challenges and understands different pains,
Her mom still sings her the same songs,
But her daughter chooses her own.
The birds keep on chirping,
She is no more a child but an adult,
She chooses to be where she wants to be,
She chooses what she wants to do,
And the mom prays for her that God would cradle her in His presence,
She wishes she was closer because of the distance,
Mom reflects that she taught her independence,
Anything that happens, whether good or bad,
Mom knows it all began with her ability to choose,
Even though at times she is not that amused,
This was her choice.

A Mother's Reflection

She has loved you, but you really didn't love her,
She has provided for you, but you only used it,
She has hugged you, but you only felt yourself,
She has cried and prayed for you to be safe.
She has shared her ups and downs with you,
but you never confided in her,
She thought you were both close, but it was an illusion.
She faced the shame,
She called on Jesus' name,
She battled to lash out and expose her heart,
What was inside of her was ugly, dirty, and cruel,
She wanted to dismiss the pain, the disappointment,
She wanted to kill the one who robbed her of her innocence,
She wanted to destroy the world he lived in,
She wanted to create a new place to live for your protection,
How could you know and not say a word?
How could you endure such a disgraceful and despicable act, and not cry to me?
She wondered,
She wondered what you learned from the Good Book,
She was broken, but she knew that only God could mend her heart again,
To forgive and move on with a smile,
How could you?

You know that I love you.
She thought you knew she would protect you.
She thought you knew,
She thought you knew that she blames herself every day,
She thought you could trust her,
She thought that you were both close.
She thought she had power to change her world,
She thought her child would have cared some more,
She thought, she thought, but it's just too late!
The mother reflected on the realities of her fate,
This mother thought and thought deeply and thought again,
She concluded that life is a reflection of imperfection.

Mediocrity

Mediocrity is a standard that is below God's blueprint,
God's Spirit causes you to want to go higher.
God Spirit in you allows you to move to a new level,
God's Spirit in you is a spirit of excellence,
It is not cheap, low, or substandard quality,
Impoverished or self-pity,
It is not mediocrity.
Every ounce of blood inside me is disgusted with mediocrity,
Every idea that I have defies the origin of mediocrity,
Every work I perform deviates from mediocrity,
Every person I embrace is above mediocrity,
Every moment I spend I combat mediocrity.
I detest the grappling experience,
Scratching like chickens on the ground, looking for some crawling worm.
I am not a chicken,
I am an eagle.
God planted a seed in the heights for me to soar,
My intention is to soar above the levels so that I can feel the high-propelling air.
They that wait upon the Lord shall renew their strength,
They shall mount up with wings as eagles, they shall run and not be weary, they shall walk and not faint.
I am an eagle ready,
I am waiting,
Running,

Mounting,
Flying,
Walking daily as God wants me to, living above Satan's schemes of mediocrity.
My strength is renewed,
I am ready to access excellence and destroy mediocrity.

I Belong to the Kingdom

I am not a commoner.
I cannot act like a commoner.
If I do I would be a counterfeit,
An imposter,
A traitor.
You and I are Kingdom children,
We belong to the King of Kings.
The Kingdom of God is yours if you accept the Kingdom of God and His righteousness.
You are royalty,
You have royal blood in your veins,
You are a royal priesthood,
A holy nation.
The Kingdom of God embraces right living,
The Kingdom of God offers blessings,
The Kingdom of God elevates to a position of leadership,
The Kingdom of God guarantees the presence of the King,
The Kingdom of God showers you with royal apparels,
The Kingdom of God provides you with jewellery of all kinds,
The Kingdom of God gives you treasures and precious stones,
The Kingdom of God sustains His children's kingdoms,
The Kingdom of God destroys all other kingdoms,
Our God reigns.

I am not an orphan.
I am not a commoner,
I am royalty,
I belong to the Kingdom of God,
I am protected by a heavenly host,
The angels of the Lord encamp round about them that fear Him.
The Kingdom of God gives me blessings that surpass the kingdom of men.
The Kingdom of God is yours if you accept the Kingdom of God and His righteousness.

Trapped

Like a bird in the cage I am living.
I want to fly away and soar to new heights.
I looked around, I felt captured, no place to soar,
Then flapping in the four corners,
My wings are growing.
The master clips them
To keep me from flying,
To make me comfortable,
To humble me, I think.
I am tired of being caged,
I want to fly, I want to soar,
I want to be able to spread my wings
Across the seas.

I feel so trapped,
I have seen the corners already.
There is more for me to explore.
I am a huge bird ready to soar,
To find new lodgings,
Be in new places,
See new faces,
Experience new adventures,
Behold new views,
Travel new journeys,
This is not news.
When I look around and see my condition,
My situation is a fact.
I am trapped!
Oh God, un-trap me!
Open my cage so I can soar.

I Am Not Trapped

I am not trapped,
I am encased with the power of God,
I break the chains that hold me!

I am not trapped,
I am enclosed with the arms that constrain me,
I break the chains that hold me!

I am not trapped,
I am encircled with the promises of God that propel me,
I break the chains that hold me!

I am not trapped,
I am embodied with the peace of God in my life,
I break the chains that hold me!

I am not trapped,
I am enveloped with the grace of God which is sufficient,
I break the chains that hold me!

I am not trapped,
I am cloaked with the righteousness of God to conquer,
I break the chains that hold me!

I am not trapped,
I am covered by the whole armour of God to fight

life's battles,
I break the chains that hold me!
I am not trapped,
I am sheltered in the house of God,
I break the chains that hold me!

You might say you are trapped,
You might think you are trapped,
Change your words,
Change your thoughts,
And be un-trapped by saying and thinking
I am not trapped!
His love constrains me.

The Rainbow's Promise

I watch the rainbow and see its beauty,
I watch the distance between us,
I gaze at its beauty from afar,
And know the beauty will be there forever.
I watch the colours and recognize diversity,
I watch the sun coming up from the horizon to kiss my face,
Then I know that there will be a change.
The rainbow will not stay forever,
But it is a reminder of a promise.
This message I could not miss,
It will never change its beauty or its distance,
This is a promise.
So I will smile when I see the rainbow and cherish the moments before the change.

Faithful Friend

I have a friend who is not near,
But everywhere I go I know she cares.
She calls me often and writes a line or ten,
She knows I love her, and I know she loves me.
Her friends are mine, mine are hers,
Our families link with ease,
We are always at peace.
I have a friend who is not near,
But for sure she is dear.

I pray for her to overcome her struggles,
I pray that God will give her health, only little troubles,
I pray that God will increase her finances,
I pray that God gives her peace in her latter days with her family.
I love my faithful friend,
She knows that I love her,
I wish that one day we will be closer, Sister P,
You are ever too true to me.

God's Eyes

God is taking record of our love today.
God's eyes look on the world, and He turns His head away,
He looks at the man He created with the dust of the earth,
He looks at the woman He created with the rib of the man,
He looks at the offspring of the human race,
And He hides his face.
He looks as his handmade fight, quarrel, hate,
God's eyes look at the
Misery of the mothers,
God's eyes look at the
Folly of the fathers,
And the cheekiness of the children.
Mothers hate their children because the fathers left them.
They hit and abuse them,
They have no mercy in what they say,
They forget the source of all things—Jesus Christ.
The fathers abandon their families and wander away to try the nectar of other women.
They show their billfolds and drive luxurious cars that sometimes are not their own.
They forget that God hears the prayers of His own.
The children cry out to the world to give them attention,
To give them true love and care.
They curse the words of the mothers and the fathers,

their first teachers and role models.
They have little or no ambition to work, so they give themselves to mischief and walk around idle.
God's eyes look,
God is taking record of our love today.
God's eyes look in the world, and He turns His head away.
He looks at the man He created with the dust of the earth,
He looks at the woman He created with the rib of the man,
He looks at the offspring of the human race,
And He hides his face.
He says, "What a disgrace!
Look at my people who are created in My image."
God's eyes look with love, so He considers marvellous grace.
He feels a deep loss so He dies on the cross to see if we will recognize His love for us.
He feels the anger and He points us to Him, the Saviour,
For us to see that He cares for us.
He looks again and remembers His commitment to man,
He writes His words to direct the way and tells us to love in spirit and in truth.
To all men, women, and youth,
God's eyes look, and He wants to see change.
He doesn't want us to be in disgrace,
But to remain constantly trusting Him until we see His face.
Friends, consider His marvellous grace.

The Gift of Love

Today is a special day.
I think of you more than ordinary,
As I see lovers across the shore,
The deep emotion is real,
I think that you have forgotten me.
Then I arrive home and there is a gift of your love,
I look at it wrapped beautifully in blues and red with a fluffy bow,
It had a picture of a heart,
And I smiled,
Feeling deeply appreciated.
My heart responded with sweet laughter and quick breaths,
You remember, oh dear, you are special.
I wonder what will be in the gift, it was surely a surprise.
The package I opened delicately,
There I found your heart wrapped in soft papers,
I held it tenderly,
Caring not to hurt you,
Drop you,
Break your heart.
I unfold, loving you more,
Your heart beats
Against my hands, and I hold you close,
Your heart beats to the rhythm of my heart,
Saying "I love you, sweetheart.
I love you, my little one.
I will cherish you today.

I will love you always.
I love you!"
Tears welled in my eyes, and I held your heart close to me,
And there I felt your breath on my face.
I drew you closer, and I felt your heart beating.
I held you tenderly,
Caring not to hurt you,
Drop you,
Break your heart.
Your heart beats to answer to my touch.
I love you, my beloved one,
I love you so much.
Thank you for the gift of love.

Love Doesn't Leave You

Love doesn't leave you,
It is you who leave love.
Love wants to stay forever,
But you think loving is a bother.
You want to move without restriction,
Love seems to be an addiction,
Love doesn't leave you,
It is you who leave love.

Love wants to come and dine with you,
But you think that the menu is the same every time.
Love wants you to know freshness and bliss,
But all you do is blow a kiss.
The kiss blows away with the wind, going in all directions.
It is not love that leaves you,
It is you who leave love.

Love wants to sleep with you,
But you think that the pillows are too hard,
And you think that the sheets are too flat.
You want to go to the soft and fluffy nests and
Stay not for long and travel again,
You want to take the nectar and settle on the flowers in different gardens.
It is not love that leaves you,
It is you who leave love.

I Pause to Say...

I pause today to think of the people I love,
And there you are in the upper chamber of my heart,
I love you today, and I know I will even love you tomorrow,
I love you in sickness, and I love you in sorrow,
I love you my friend.
I know our relationship will not end.
I pause to say you are very special to me,
In my dreams we are all free.
I think of the moments we share in laughter,
I think of the doubts we had about each other,
I think of the moments we wait in silence,
I think of the days we write and read messages from each other,
I think of the singing and the glancing and the smiling, the knowing that you are there.
I pause to say in those moments I had no fear.
I pause to say the time will come when we will experience fun times again.
I pause to say if it does not happen again, I will preserve the memories as keepsakes in my heart.

His Clear Voice

I hear His voice distinctly clear.
I heard the huskiness, the resonance, oh so rare.
He says the words so fluently, rolling like liquid over a rock.
He speaks with purpose, his pitch, his tone, just right.
His voice is music to my ears,
If he whispers, there is an excited shiver,
If He shouts there is powerful awareness,
I hear His voice anywhere,
I know it anywhere.
It is distinctly clear.

I Will See You Later

I look in your eyes and understand what love is,
Love is really a truth that shouldn't be denied.
I sighed peacefully,
Then time tells me it's time to go,
I felt a tug of deep pain to let go.
I wanted to stay close to you,
To hear you,
To listen to you,
To admire you,
To know you more,
But soon I have to close the door.

I have to go, I cannot tell you how I feel.

I will not say goodbye, I will see you later.
I hate to tell you I am not going to see you
Because there is an empty place,
I feel so lonely across the miles without you.
I will not say goodbye,
I will say, "See you later."
I look in your eyes and understand what love is,
Love is really a truth that shouldn't be denied.
I sighed peacefully,
I will see you later.

When I See Him Again: A Young love Story

When I see him
My heart skips a beat,
I feel flush and a great surge of heat,
I look away and moisten my lips,
My heart keeps pounding like a conga drum.
I try to sing, but it diminishes to an unsteady hum,
What would I say?
Lord, I feel like a fool, I really do not know how to maintain my cool.
Oh God, he is coming near.
Perfect love has no fear,
But what will he think of me?
I love him and I have to pretend
That I am as strong as can be,
Oh God, what is happening to me?
"Hi," he said,
I know I should reply but my voice is stuck in my head.
I bend my head and mumble some words, talking to my heart.
I look up with a bright smile and say a prayer to God to keep me smart.
I know that I love him. I know it in my mind and heart.
It doesn't make sense to pretend,
God, my heart You can apprehend,
Only You can comprehend,
He is a friend.
A true friend is very rare,

The Good Book says,
A friend loveth at all times—
Through sickness, mistakes, failures, and imperfections,
A friend will know, too, of the connections.
Love covers a multitude of sins.
I can only be human and nothing else,
So I will love, dream, and be free,
Because love triggers different emotions in us.
There is no need to cry and fuss,
I will not feel fear,
I will not feel pain,
I have no need to pretend
When I see him again.
He is a friend.

Be Aware

Be aware that people are not what they seem to be,
Be aware that everyone does not have your best interest,
Be aware that not everyone cares about you and wants you to succeed,
Be aware that only you can stop your progress,
Be aware that within you there is power,
Be aware that you can access opportunities this very hour,
Be aware that not everyone who smiles with you is your friend,
Be aware that people cannot take you where they have not been,
Be aware that people cannot make you be when you have a will,
Be aware that every time you make a mistake it is to teach you a lesson,
Be aware that you can move forward and fight to be released from life's prison,
Be aware that you are the only one that will give God an account for your duties,
Be aware that you have built-in potential that can promote you to excellence,
Be aware that true friends are precious and that they are rare,
Be aware that you should not strive to be vain and addicted to fear,
Be aware that sometimes you will feel alone but you

are not really alone,
Be aware as you progress you will find new ways to deal with people,
Be aware that there is always good and there is always evil,
Be aware that when you grow you will experience changes,
Be aware that you can make the difference based on your choices,
Be aware that if you do not learn you really do not care.

If You Are in Love

If you are in love with the wrong person,
If you are in love with the wrong thing,
If you are in love with the wrong system,
If you are in love with the wrong principles,
If you are in love with the wrong values,
If you are in love with the wrong master,
If you are in love without the Creator,
You will have to work double time,
Triple time,
An eternity to accomplish your true identity,
To maximize your God-given creativity,
To realize your dreams.
If you are in love with the wrong whatever,
You are going to pay for it forever,
The consequences are bound to come!
Therefore, guard your heart to love right,
It is not going to be easy,
But be ready with God's power to fight.

Rhythms of Culture

Rhythms of Culture

Culture comes in the rhythms of the drums,
Culture comes in the songs and the hums,
Culture comes in the rhythms of the dance,
Culture comes in the wild jolly prance,
Culture comes in the rhythms of cuisines,
Culture comes in the natural scenes,
Culture has a rhythm of its own,
Culture gives everyone something to own.

Culture's rhythms are powerful,
At this moment I am quite wilful.
Culture causes me to learn of you,
Culture causes me to dance with you,
Culture causes me to sing with you,
Culture causes me to understand you,
Culture causes me to eat with you,
Culture causes me to travel with you,
Culture causes me to dress with you,
Culture causes me not to judge you,
Culture causes me to find you,
Culture causes me to love you,
Culture defines who you are,
In your country,
In your home,
In your church,
In your school.

Culture causes peace and war,
Culture celebrates diversity,
Culture stimulates creativity,
The rhythms of culture beat in me!

Church People Have Different Faces

Even the people in church have different faces,
They behave differently.
I am not talking about being changed by the blood of Jesus,
I am reflecting that an unsaved is a new creation,
I am considering the change of the nature to be sinful,
I am saying that church people are carnal, brutish, and mean.
Today they smile with you, the next day they frown,
The next day they pass you like you are a stranger,
The next day you are a foreigner,
The next day they hug you,
The next day they bug you,
The next day they eat with you, the next day they beat you,
The next day they sing with you, the next day they sting you,
The next day they dine with you, the next day they decline from you.
There are many who are blocked from knowing Christ based on our actions.
We talk about our church brothers and sisters with our unsaved family members and wonder why they are not coming to church to listen to the pastor.
I pray that church will stop having fake people,
But I remember the Good Book says that the wheat and tares have to grow together until the day of harvest,

So I want to encourage all church people to stop being bench warmers,
Being hypocrites,
And be Kingdom children who are true worshippers.
Let us stop pretending and playing church because we cannot fool God,
He is all-knowing.
The people in church have different faces,
I am not talking about putting on powder-based makeup that can be washed off.
Maybe that's it!
We wear too many masks in church,
We can change the shade and the colour to please ourselves.
Today they clap for you, the next day they stop,
The next day they are happy with you, the next day they are sad,
The next day they wink at you, the next day they are blind to you,
The people in church have different faces,
Look in the mirror and do not change!

Behold Your Sins Shall Find You Out

I trusted people as they confessed Christ,
I found that most, if not all, are not nice,
They pretend to love and care,
And deep in their hearts they are not fair,
They are so subtle, they even give Satan a scare,
Behold, your sin shall find you out.
They would pray and lift holy hands and make great, strong shouts,
They would counsel and grin with you looking very pious,
They would tell you of visions and dreams that make you quiver,
They would visit and call when they are looking for something,
They would give impressions that are bound to fade out,
Behold, your sin shall find you out.
They are worse than the wicked criminals who are behind bars,
I pray that God will take away all my scars,
One day, one day, you will not escape because your sin is coming out,
You are going to try to hide, but everything will be revealed,
Because in your heart you want only to steal,
I pray for you that His vengeance you will appeal.
Behold, your sin shall find you out.
I will pray to God for you to know that what we do for people is not for show,

When I love I mean inside out, and I purpose in my heart that the world will know
That sin has a way of uncovering itself and bringing light to situations again,
Be careful, my friends, God is awake when I am asleep,
And as I am sure, there is a day and a night,
Behold, your sin shall find you out.

Oh God, We Are Guilty

Oh God, we are guilty of disrespecting authority, yet we want to lead God's people to Him.
Oh God, we are guilty for slaughtering and murdering God's people with our tongues, yet we lift our hands and shout praises to God.
We are guilty of dealing with people like they are machines, yet we want others to consider our human nature.
We are guilty of omitting and neglecting opportunities to evangelize others, yet we look for every chance to excel.
We are guilty of robbing God by refraining from giving tithes and offerings, yet we are asking for financial blessings.
We are guilty of treating our family and friends with more respect than God's servant, yet we are concerned why people make things difficult for us.
We are guilty of watching every other people's business, yet we have a lot of mess in our own homes and lives.
We are guilty of acting like we are super humans, yet we are asking for wisdom to be healthy and prosperous.
We are guilty of building other people's missions, yet we are wondering why there is no growth in ours.
We are guilty of observing our business above God's, yet we are wondering why our business does not flourish consistently.
We are guilty of being gluttonous for things that feed

our desires, yet we sing, "This is my desire to honour you, God."

We are guilty of expecting changes from within, yet we resist change by our attitudes and our voices.

We are guilty of acting like we are perfect, yet God's Word says there is none perfect, no, not one.

We are guilty for saying we want unity to go to Heaven, yet we are divided by labels and cannot tolerate each other on Earth.

Oh God, we are guilty because we neglect to use love as a verb instead of a noun.

We are guilty of not being honest about where we stand with God, yet we speak, sing, and preach without God's anointing on our lives.

We are guilty of blocking sinners from coming to our church, yet we say we are witnesses to the world.

We are guilty of more things that I am not inspired to say.

We are guilty before God our Saviour, it is time to pray.

Thank God we can be innocent now as we apply God's sufficient grace.

What else are we guilty of?

Only we and God know that we are guilty of not taming our tongues

And loving others as He taught,

I asked God to forgive me,

Will you do that, too?

Do it now when He is your Saviour, the next time He might be your judge.

The Girl, Diamond, Next Door
In Jamaican Dialect

There was a girl next door who has
Many curls, she is beautiful and all the boys in the community bet to get her pearl.
She smiles up with Dick, Tom, and Harry, never knowing that their heart is fickle.
She feels good when she gets lunch money,
She buys all kind of things, and brags and boasts to everybody.
Dick says, "I love you so quick."
Harry says, "Please give me in a hurry."
Tom says, "I love you," and squeezes her palm.
Everyone bets on who can get Diamond's pearl first,
They know that Diamond wants to be a nurse.

One day, without them knowing, she heard them talking all in one place,
She hid behind the bushes and when they described what they would do to her,
She was red with hot flushes,
She blushed,
She was embarrassed,
She felt like she was in prison.
After contemplating her new revelation,
She decided to play with them a little to teach them a lesson.
She dressed up nicely in pants and a long coat,
And went with each of them in a crowded boat,
She invited her friends to come with her on their dates,

She talked and talked about Dick,
She talked about Tom,
She talked about Harry,
She talked to each of them about their proposals,
And brought much more confusion.

Everyone tried to win Diamond's heart,
And you and I know they want to pull her skirt,
"What do you want to do, my love?
 I will help you to accomplish your goals
 If you give me a chance to sail you to the moon."
"No, my dear, you are my own. I sleep and dream that you were in white."
"My love is real. I have a ring to show you. Come to me, I don't bite."
Diamond listened to all three and wondered which was true.
Tom said, "Come far to the mountains to nurse my wounds."
Harry said, "My precious one, you have a perfect nose."
Dick said, "Here are yellow flowers, my sunshine, for you my deary, I cannot help myself, let me pick your berry."
Then Diamond looked at the old good fi nothing fool, who want a quickie to cool him tool,
Tom who want to sink her goals, and Harry who mouth a drool with old age,
And said, "I really do not understand what is on your page."
She waited for them to be together where everyone could see her face clear,
"Dick, you are not free, you have a wife,"
"Tom, you need to have a trade,"
"Harry, no chance for you, go mine your pickney!"

Diamond took from her pocket their taped voices,
And revealed the truth to their faces,
And said, "Imagine, I cannot be none of you wife,"
She got brave and acknowledged her mistake
Of being played by three old gruffs,
She thought that was enough.
Diamond eyes sparkled with fire and with rage
For everyone in the neighbourhood to witness rampage.
When the crowd came from their holes like a swarm of bees,
Dick, Tom, and Harry felt so ashamed and ran way with the breeze,
The woman dem laugh and told Diamond that she must shine,
And sparkle in spirit and soul and in her mind.
The community encouraged her to be wise in her choices to accomplish her goal,
One old Christian woman warned, "The devil always send a trap fi possess your soul."

Shifted Rear

In Jamaican Dialect

Mi dear me a go fi exercise as usual at Keep Fit when me see a strange happening
That everyone in the room couldn't miss,
Imagine de woman come fi exercise with her false posterior,
All a wi eyes couldn't lef her bottom.
The man dem eyes dem follow her as she move on the treadmill,
Me a wonder a wha' so wrong wid we if we cyaan catch no eye,
Den me look, a bottom looking back at me, looking quite funny,
Me couldn't keep it in, me seh, "A wha dis ya?"
All a we eye start follow the machine effect from behind,
No, we were not thinking anything but to see where the shifted false bottom was going,
One was up and the other was down.
Maybe it was doing the electric slide,
I couldn't help but ask fi excuse because all me laughter come up fi choke me.
The woman stand up right in front a mi,
I was tempted fi hole di shifted rear and put it in place.
I look at it again, den look pon her face,
Some seh, "Woman, look behind you."
There she was looking pon me,
Want me fi feel like a me crazy,

I thought her posterior had risen or the miracle fat them melt off,
Imagine de woman put on false bottom fe fool we that she had a fat butt.
Instead the woman clap her behind down on the floor,
She kissed her teeth, cut her eye, and ready fi gwan like me shouldn't deh deh,
I seh to mi self, "I wonder a who she tink a prekay,"
So me tun and tell her in a whisper,
She kiss her teeth and try fi mek me feel inferior.
"Woman, yuh behind shift!
It is missing the right place.
From my angle, it match yuh face."
She was angry beyond control, by then me deh pon the ground a roll,
What a thing, I tink you would wear false bottom in jeans
Fi look sexy on a date with your special someone,
In a dress, or fi just add some good looks to your posterior.

"Shift it over to the right side, Miss, go to di bathroom,
Okay, stay deh, your false bottom move fi you fi exercise with ease."
The woman face get so red, a know she wasn't pleased,
So before she get more upset, I said,
"I think you should go to the bathroom and check your posterior."
I know this woman was at the gym fi de wrong reason,
You nuh come here fi tek off fat, yuh come fi find a person,
Si deh you bottom fat melt off and shift because of the exercise.

De look she give me was for my demise,
Same time mi move from behind her and go up front de exercise class,
No more was I going to shield her and her shifted ass.
Everyone seemed to be shocked till no words could come,
She pack her tings fas like a jet and ran out with her lean bottom,
Upward bottom, shaking, shifted rear,
We look at each other in the room,
Me tell you the whole class ketch a fire,
We hoop, we laugh, and wallow on the ground, none a we care.
As we exercise and someone remember
Or see a behind moving on a machine,
We only hear a snicker, then a roar of laughter.
All the stress we had dat day melt away,
Like the shifted rear that couldn't stay,
Friends, me still a wonder which one of the exercise machine was made to take the fat off her false rear.

Cockroach Nuh Business in a Fowl Fight

In Jamaican Dialect

I have learnt from the past that when people are fighting over power,
Leave them alone,
Because most times they are not fighting the system, but they are fighting each other.
I know that everyone is my brother and everyone is my sister,
I have learnt that when they fight each other to rule their dynasty,
They don't have ears to hear or think through my philosophy,
So I just listen and do what I can 'cause my granny usually seh to me,
"Cockroach nuh business in a fowl fight."
In other words, you should keep out a family or friend or same people business
Weh yu nuh belong,
Because dem wi nyam you!
Dem wi bond together and alienate you,
Dem wi kill you.
Learn that lesson. Yuh hear me tell you?
If a woman come to me fi complain
Bout har mate or lover,
Mi jus listen to har fi di hour,
Because me know that everything change when dem under cover.
When she hear di nice words of her lover and is influenced under intimate power,

She figet di ting she vex bout, and if me remind har she tek me fi intruder.
Cockroach nuh business in a fowl fight, remember!
Sometimes me watch likkle pickney get bex wid each other,
And as soon as dem get together fi play with a toy or be on the playground
You have to wonder, dem act like peas inna pod.
I don't mind dem because dem know fi apalagize and forget the business of hate and confusion,
But I tell you, the adults dem who always want to kick out dem own people fi get on top,
Me nuh have nutten fi seh,
Mi nuh business inna family cass cass,
Remember me tell you seh cockroach nuh business in a fowl fight,
Do not intervene in another person's business because dem wi kill you.
Me learn dat if you find it hard to keep your mouth quiet, jus groan and roll your tongue,
Not a word you should seh because cockroach nuh business in a fowl fight.

Gossip

In Jamaican Dialect

Him seh she seh, but weh him did seh?
Him seh she seh, no a him seh, but weh you seh?
That is the story we neva hear.
I am weary of people who gossip.
I wish I could slap them on their lip.
I wonder if they really don't know what truth is.
I open my heart to love, but as soon as I see that is garbage you bring, I move away
Because I have a purpose to fulfill,
I have to speak what God wants me to,
So move out of my way.
Weh yuh seh him seh? She seh a nuh so him seh,
A pure she seh,
I wonder weh you seh.
The same way you find time to talk about someone else who used to be your frien',
It is the same way yu will talk me.
I really throw weh garbage, I am not a garbage collector,
Gossip stinks, and very soon I will be carrying news,
Saying him seh, she seh, and wouldn't seh what me did seh.
A matter a fact I might not even remember weh me did seh.
Then we would get in a prekay, lie, gossip, carry-go-bring-come, tale-bearing,
All ah it boil right down to sin.
Me prefer fi gossip the gospel,
To tell someone about Jesus and weh Him do fi me.

I don't have to mek it up or tell lie because He is the truth and the life,
So when you come wid yuh gossip and you hear silence, or you hear me start sing
Or change the argument or walk way, it's yuh mout.
Too much gossip 'bout people is a danger alarm fi all.
It is not what God expec' from we Christians at all.

Rhythms of the Park

Inspired by Urban Development Corporation (UDC)
Environment project at New Day Primary School in Jamaica

Beat the drum slowly,
The rhythms of the park,
It is very dark,
The park is very dark,
The park needs a spark.
We feel sad at New Day
Because the Grants Pen Peace Park
Wants to laugh, wants to cry,
Wants to live, and wants to be clean.
The earth makes a sigh to the passersby
Who want a place to rest their weary feet,
To relax, read, watch a game, and be free, safe, and happy,
The park needs us to work together to build our community.

Raise the beats of the drums,
Make it lively and sweet,
There is a new day at New Day,
We are feeling glad, feeling good,
There is a spark in the park,
Feeling bold at New Day,
Because we worked on Grants Pen Peace Park for it to be renovated.
The garden wants to laugh, wants to cry, and wants to live,
It is no more polluted,
The CHASE sign says "Hi" to the passersby.
We see mother earth, flowers, and happy seats,

For the young and the old
Who want to rest their weary feet,
To relax, read, meet, watch a game and be free, safe, and happy.
The park is now clean.
UDC, thank you for the opportunity to work in the Grants Peace community.
Did you know the renovation will continue to grow?
I hope everyone in the community will keep their surroundings clean and make it pleasant to the eyes.
I hope individuals will ensure their parks are inviting,
And that they would have ongoing projects in clubs to support the maintenance of beautification
And restoration of parks and community centres.
There are many who do not have sufficient space at home but depend on the municipality
To create pleasant places for relaxation,
So everyone will feel happy every day.

Gullies Cry

Inspired by the passing of a student & UDC environment project–Gully Care

The gullies cry, the gullies cry, the gullies cry,
And all the people around a wonder why
The gullies cry.

The gullies cry because the garbage stinks,
The huge and small rats infest the areas,
The cockroaches crawl everywhere,
Mosquitoes get a chance to multiply,
The gullies cry and the people around wonder why.

The gullies cry because our children get diseases of different kinds,
Typhoid, dengue, cholera, gastroenteritis, leptospirosis, diarrhea.
The gullies cry because the people blame the government.
They say, "We want justice," when they are responsible.
The gullies cry at their ignorance and wish they could give assistance.

The gullies cry, the gullies cry, the gullies cry,
And the people around a wonder why
The gullies cry.

The gullies cry because people build houses on them.
They dig too deep beside them and weaken their sides and tear them away.

When the flood comes,
The gully walls cannot take the weight of the house and the pangs from the water at the same time.
The gully at Sandy Park and Grants Pen collapsed and left a sad history behind.
Student Boyd, our student and his family, met sudden demise.
The school community wishes that all will be wise,
The community cries and the gully cries,
The community cries because their loved one was washed away.

The gullies look at the people who build on their banks and sighed, "What a pity."
They need to understand that the gullies have a life and must keep them alive.
The gullies need their walls to be firmly intact with no rubbish inside.
The gullies cry because they cannot find free course to travel.
The gullies cry when they see people being washed away by the torrents of water, helplessly.

The gullies cry, the gullies cry, the gullies cry
The gullies cry, the gullies cry, the gullies cry
And the people around a wonder why
The gullies cry.

The gullies cry and look away when persons cry for their families,
The gullies cry when they see small corpses hitched in debris,
The gullies cry when persons are killed because they lived carelessly,
And they are gone in the spread of the seas.

The gullies cry, "Protect us, we have a purpose!"
The gullies cry, "Don't build your houses on us!
Keep us clean!
Care for us!"
The gullies cry!

Nothing You Say or Do

You cannot stop me.
Nothing you say can move me to tears.
Nothing you do can change my heart to go forward.
Nothing you try will be able to derail me.
Nothing you plan for me will cause me to change.
Nothing you try to convince me of will shelf my idea.
Nothing you do can stop me from going.
Nothing you do will stop me from being.
Nothing you sing can charm my heart to flutter.
Nothing you say can allow me to forget my roots.
Nothing you say will cause me to forget who I am.
Nothing you say will change my perspectives.
Nothing you say will cause me not to want to live.
Nothing you say will keep me in darkness.
Nothing you do will keep me from progressing.
Nothing you do will keep me listening.
Nothing you do will keep me trusting.
Nothing you do will keep me drooling.
NOTHING.

Simply nothing you do or say can move me to go
Below the standards of where I am inspired to be.
Everything I do is to be a better me.

I Want To

I want to multiply me
To the children I meet.
I want to multiply me to the teachers.
I want to multiply me to the women.
I want to multiply me.
I have one life to live.
I know we are uniquely different.
I know that when I die there will not be another me,
So today, even though I cannot do math much,
I want to multiply me.
I want to leave a legacy behind
For my favourite people, children, women, and parents,
There are so many things I want to say to you.

To children: remember to obey your parents,
Respect them always,
Never forget positive values and attitudes,
And never seek your own pleasures when they are displeasing to God.
Find someone mature and God-fearing to guide you.
Trust God with all your heart and study wisely, and work to achieve your goals.

To women: ensure you have a skill.
Empower yourself and do not be shadowed by your friends and mate.
Think for yourself and do not depend on your friends to make decisions for you.

Work hard to achieve and think about life positively.
Never let the negative experiences cause you to be less than,
Find positive friends and do not spend time on gossip,
Only let kind thoughts and words come from your lips.

Parents: you are blessed to have children.
Do not spoil them because they are lovely.
Do not make them your idol.
Trust God to help you to deal with each of them differently because they are never the same.
Consider their feelings and do not seek to be their chummy friends,
Because you cannot be, you are their parents!
You parents should guide with love and always speak the truth to your children, even if it hurts,
Because when you do not, they think you are approving of their deeds.
Always be honest because your children will model you.
When they make their decisions that you do not agree with,
Leave them and wait for them to learn from their situations
Because each child has his own ideals and will falter.
Let us as parents rest assured that we have nurtured in love and discipline.
I want to let you know that each of us, wherever we are,
Whatever we do, we affect someone on our way.
Therefore, let us strive for excellence in our attitude and pray.

Break the Silence
In Memory of a student

Numbed in silence,
Such a gruesome act.
No one bridled their tongue,
Each forgot about tact.
We cried in pain, heaviness was our meal,
We cried and prayed that no pain we would feel.
We prayed and waited for our good Lord to intervene,
And wondered why He didn't stop the dismal scene,
Where a student was raped, killed, and left naked to searching eyes,
No time for your family or friends to say good bye.
She was a girl of promise, who gave her heart to the Lord,
A pathfinder in the Adventist church,
An ardent camper and youth at Jessups Sunday church,
A past student of our primary and secondary school.

There are so many versions of what actually happened.
One thing for sure was that she was going to church—Mannings Hill Adventist,
The rain started to fall and she did not want to get wet,
She ran for shelter at her alma mater, all out of breath.
In her mind she was thinking of the Sabbath school,
Her Pathfinders friends, and memorizing her Bible verses from beginning to end.

She was so absorbed in looking for a bus, thinking that the time was getting late,
Not knowing that sheltering at her primary school would be her fate.
As she looked up her atmosphere was changed,
Charged in the air was the spirit of rape,
An unscrupulous, wicked demon snatched the heart of a man or men,
I wish there was a videotape.
His intent was to rob, kill, and destroy, and not think of the nation above self.
Such crime seared an ugly scar on our minds, in our hearts, and brought heaviness to our soul.
Many of us were numb beyond words to speak.
We even imagined the ordeal that the student could feel,
Just our imaginations strangled our spirit, making us weak.
Her innocence was ravished from her,
Wet blood clung to her hot flesh,
Her head and inner-body ached,
She railed and cried,
Sobbed and squealed,
It was a disaster, an immoral earthquake.
The time ticked away,
She remembered her Bible verse,
And missed the last moments of her memories,
Moving from lateness to dead silence.
No mortal was there to save her from violence,
So her Saviour and Father cradled her in His comforting presence.

Now our student was silenced from telling her story, but I know her demise was not in vain.
Because each of us can feel the pain,
We can show solidarity and unity,

Let every child be our responsibility.
If we remain silent, we are destroying the future of the nation.
We need to speak out to truly honour and celebrate the life of our student.
Let us work together to stop the violence and crime against children.
If you know something or someone who is involved in crime,
TODAY, not tomorrow, is the time to stop being just numb,
And break the silence!

Tribute to My Mentor, My Queen, Dr. Josette Smikle

I have a mentor, who was my tutor,
She was an educator extraordinaire
Who loved in abundance like a millionaire.
She loved to chuckle,
She was Dr. Smikle,
She was never idle.
Everyone who did Literacy Studies at UWI
Will say, "Lecturer Smikle a fi wi."
She was really loving to all,
She never tried to let her students look small.
She found every opportunity to make us soar, and made sacrifices beyond the shores.
She had a pout and sometimes I wondered what to say to her,
But as I drew near I felt her soul and not long after, I became bold.
I knew she loved with all her heart,
And I felt sad to know from her I must part.
I prayed and thought of my mentor,
Many times she asked about my daughter,
She wanted to make our family better.
She adopted her students' families as hers,
And made sure we excelled wherever we go,
She was a proud mom as she watched us grow.

She shared email messages to inspire and encourage us.
She cared if you and I made progress.

She was not selfish and mean.
Smikle was and still is my dream.
She is and will always be my mentor, my queen.
She was royalty in her dress, she donned her hair in curls and braids,
She put on stylish earrings that matched her necklace,
She wore brown, green, hues of cream, and all the earth tones.
We talked about issues in the education system, challenges, and dreams.
She never showed a tinge of carnal pride, but showed how proud she was when we achieved.
She covered our limitations with her wings and talked privately to us for us to improve.
She said, "Cynthia," in her kind, sweet voice, "you can make it, just keep doing what's right."
She told me when I fussed about my middle name that my name has a rhythm.
She gave me counsel to keep following Him,
I believed in her, she believed in me, her welfare mattered so much to me.
Though she is no more to be seen in this my world.
I see her in every letter, word, sentence, and literature,
I see her in the sea, the birds, the trees, in nature,
I hold her passion in my heart to change my world through literacy.
I think God put her in my life for a reason,
And today, again, I cherish her memory.
I thank you, my mother, educator, counsellor, sister, friend Smikle,
I promise I will do everything you want to hear your chuckle.
You are my mentor, my queen.

Tribute to Myles Munroe
Written November 9, 2014 (the day he passed)

Yesterday you were here, but today you are not.
You were taken away suddenly, in a FLASH!
You were sent to Heaven with a plane crash.
The crash thought you were crushed, but our memories of you are alive,
You left such a beautiful and remarkable legacy behind.
Sleep on, my brother, sleep on, sleep on,
Your name will be on our lips forever.
You are gone like the wind in the summer,
But as the sun shines we reflect in a whisper.
The sun shines brighter as we listen about your ministries,
As we listen as your people,
We listen to your stories,
As we read your eulogy,
We want to make an apology,
We wish we had stopped to tell you more that we love you,
That we appreciate your counsel,
That we appreciate your messages,
That you are our hero, mentor,
Our teacher, motivator, and friend.
Because you have been that to so many others,
I just pray that others would have told you before your end.

A Look at Death

Death came and left us numb.
Death came and took our sister away.
Death came and shattered our dreams.
Death captures our love and causes them to scream.
Death comes and whispers to our loved ones and steals their heart away.
Death moves us to think of our realities.
Death moves us to consider only miseries.
Death propels us to move to a better life.
Death takes our daughter and his wife.
Death cherishes our son and her husband.
Death massages our egos to love the bond.
Death tells us to sing because she goes to a better land.
Death helps us to see that death has power to transport
To a place of stillness,
A place of worship,
A place of hopelessness,
A place of doom,
A place of peace,
Death calls,
Who will answer?

The Power of Death

Death is powerful.
It knows how to capture us to keep us still.
Death takes his toes.
Death climbs to his feet so he could not run.
Death searches him and reaches his stomach.
Death pricks his lungs and lets the air seep out slowly.
Death knocks his heart and the rhythms change dynamics to low and high, then stillness.
Death leaves him dead to the sound of the wind.
Death leaves him dead to the beauty of the ocean.
Death leaves him dead to the cries of his friends.
Death leaves him dead to the groaning of his family.
Death leaves him dead to the eulogy of his life.
Death leaves him dead to the preaching of the pastor.
Death leaves him dead to the expectations of tomorrow.
Death leaves him to the coldness of earth.
Death leaves him dead.
Death is really powerful.

Dying

Dying is making space for another.
Dying is creating a moment to celebrate a brother or sister.
Dying is marshalling families to be united with each other.
Dying is shifting focus to friends to see the needs of one another.
Dying is harmonizing people to reflect on the Superior Being.
Dying is plucking the best people to be a spirit for our memories.
Dying is enlightening to the listeners to give them hope to prepare their destinies.
Dying is spreading to the nation a message that we need one another.
Dying is giving us a chance to make things right with our neighbour.
Dying is for us to make a difference in nature.
Dying is transporting us to a better place from the living.
Dying is resting with hope.

My Prayer

Father in Heaven, Father of my life,
You are awesome, there is none like You!
I praise You for the blessings You have given to me
And for the promises You shared with me.
You promise never to leave me, so I believe You are right here in me, around me, beside me.
Your Word says, "Lo, I am with you always, even unto the end of the earth."
Oh my Lord, Saviour, and friend, this is so comforting.
Father God, my desire is to have Your strength to cope with life's realities,
Let me not be influenced by the wickedness around me.
Let me not be encouraged to do anything that does not please You.
Let me embrace the mean, the wicked, and the indifferent ones with Your love.
Let me be conscious of my purpose on Earth and see Your visions above.
Enrich my life so that Your will for me will be easy to accept.
Teach me patience to live in my realities.
Teach me longsuffering to cope with my calamities.
Teach me peace to deal with each situation.
Teach me love to continue to be an inspiration.
Oh God, I love You so much.
Your approval means everything to me.
I will yet praise you for my family and friends.
Oh God, give me a heart to serve you sincerely from

now until life ends.
Equip me to be that agent of change and allow me to be focused and not distracted
To fulfill Your call on my life.
Help me, oh God, to be a great person,
An excellent educator,
And a committed wife,
Trusting you.
Do what it takes to make me true, for Heaven is where I want to be.
Thank you, Jesus, that all power is given unto me to be what You want me to be.
Keep me true and glorify Yourself through me.
Allow me to see Your doors open and walk confidently through them to fulfill Your purpose.
Teach me to be humble and to wait patiently on You.
I ask all these things in Your name.
Hallelujah! Hallelujah! Hallelujah!
Amen.

www.ingramcontent.com/pod-product-compliance
Lightning Source LLC
Chambersburg PA
CBHW070202100426
42743CB00013B/3011